EXAMINING ISSUES THROUGH
POLITICAL CARTOONS

The Great Depression

Titles in the Examining Issues Through Political Cartoons series
include:

Abortion
Censorship
Civil Rights
The Death Penalty
The Environment
Euthanasia
The Great Depression
Illegal Immigration
Iraq
The Nazis
Terrorism
Watergate

Examining Issues Through
POLITICAL CARTOONS

The Great
Depression

Edited by William Dudley

Bonnie Szumski, *Publisher*
Scott Barbour, *Managing Editor*

GREENHAVEN
PRESS®

THOMSON

———————★———TM

GALE

San Diego • Detroit • New York • San Francisco • Cleveland
New Haven, Conn. • Waterville, Maine • London • Munich

THOMSON
——————★——————™
GALE

© 2004 by Greenhaven Press. Greenhaven Press is an imprint of The Gale Group, Inc., a division of Thomson Learning, Inc.

Greenhaven® and Thomson Learning™ are trademarks used herein under license.

For more information, contact
Greenhaven Press
27500 Drake Rd.
Farmington Hills, MI 48331-3535
Or you can visit our Internet site at http://www.gale.com

LIBRARY OF CONGRESS CATALOGING-IN-PUBLICATION DATA

The Great Depression / William Dudley, book editor.
    p. cm. — (Examining issues through political cartoons)
Includes bibliographical references and index.
ISBN 0-7377-1253-8 (pbk. : alk. paper) — ISBN 0-7377-1254-6 (lib. : alk. paper)
    1. United States—Politics and government—1933–1945—Caricatures and cartoons. 2. Depression—1929—United States—Caricatures and cartoons.
3. American wit and humor, Pictorial. 4. Editorial cartoons—United States.
I. Dudley, William, 1964–   . II. Series.

E806.G828 2004
973.91'6'0222—dc22

                                                                    2003049496

Printed in the United States of America

Contents

Foreword   6

Introduction   8

Chapter 1: The Depression Sets In   21
  Preface   22

Chapter 2: President Hoover Responds   32
  Preface   33

Chapter 3: Business Versus Labor
          in the Great Depression   41
  Preface   42

Chapter 4: Roosevelt's New Deal   50
  Preface   51

Chronology   66

For Further Research   71

Index   75

Foreword

Political cartoons, also called editorial cartoons, are drawings that do what editorials do with words—express an opinion about a newsworthy event or person. They typically appear in the opinion pages of newspapers, sometimes in support of that day's written editorial, but more often making their own comment on the day's events. Political cartoons first gained widespread popularity in Great Britain and the United States in the 1800s when engravings and other drawings skewering political figures were fashionable in illustrated newspapers and comic magazines. By the beginning of the 1900s, editorial cartoons were an established feature of daily newspapers. Today, they can be found throughout the globe in newspapers, magazines, and online publications and the Internet.

Art Wood, both a cartoonist and a collector of cartoons, writes in his book *Great Cartoonists and Their Art:*

> Day in and day out the cartoonist mirrors history; he reduces complex facts into understandable and artistic terminology. He is a political commentator and at the same time an artist.

The distillation of ideas into images is what makes political cartoons a valuable resource for studying social and historical topics. Editorial cartoons have a point to express. Analyzing them involves determining both what the cartoon's point is and how it was made.

Sometimes, the point made by the cartoon may be one that the reader disagrees with, or considers offensive. Such cartoons expose readers to new ideas and thereby challenge them to analyze and question their own opinions and assumptions. In some extreme cases, cartoons provide vivid examples of the thoughts that lie behind heinous acts; for example, the cartoons created by the Nazis illustrate the anti-Semitism that led to the mass persecution of Jews.

Examining controversial ideas is but one way the study of political cartoons can enhance and develop critical thinking skills. Another aspect to cartoons is that they can use symbols to make their point quickly. For example, in a cartoon in *Euthanasia*, Chuck Asay depicts supporters of a legal "right to die" by assisted suicide as vultures. Vultures are birds that eat dead and dying animals and are often a symbol of repulsive and cowardly predators who take advantage of those who have met misfortune or are vulnerable. The reader can infer that Asay is expressing his opposition to physician-assisted suicide by suggesting that its supporters are just as loathsome as vultures. Asay thus makes his point through a quick symbolic association.

An important part of critical thinking is examining ideas and arguments in their historical context. Political cartoonists (reasonably) assume that the typical reader of a newspaper's editorial page already has a basic knowledge of current issues and newsworthy people. Understanding and appreciating political cartoons often requires such knowledge, as well as a familiarity with common icons and symbolic figures (such as Uncle Sam's representing the United States). The need for contextual information becomes especially apparent in historical cartoons. For example, although most people know who Adolf Hitler is, a lack of familiarity with other German political figures of the 1930s may create difficulty in fully understanding cartoons about Nazi Germany made in that era.

Providing such contextual information is one important way that Greenhaven's Examining Issues Through Political Cartoons series seeks to make this unique and revealing resource conveniently accessible to students. Each volume presents a representative and diverse collection of political cartoons focusing on a particular current or historical topic. An introductory essay provides a general overview of the subject matter. Each cartoon is then presented with accompanying information including facts about the cartoonist and information and commentary on the cartoon itself. Finally, each volume contains additional informational resources, including listings of books, articles, and websites; an index; and (for historical topics) a chronology of events. Taken together, the contents of each anthology constitute an amusing and informative resource for students of historical and social topics.

Introduction

For millions of Americans in the year 1929, the future looked bright. It had been more than a decade since American soldiers had returned home from Europe and the "war to end all wars." The United States since then had witnessed exciting advances in technology, unprecedented material prosperity, and social exuberance as America's "flaming youth" experimented with new ideas of living, drinking, dressing, and sexuality. Almost half of all Americans owned their own homes; two-thirds had electric power. Millions of Americans discovered new consumer pleasures, including touring in automobiles, listening to sports events and shows on the radio, and going to motion pictures.

Much of the optimism Americans felt was predicated on the economy, which had rebounded from World War I and a brief 1920 recession to experience unprecedented growth. Between 1921 and 1929 America's industrial output almost doubled. Unemployment remained between 2 and 3 percent. New inventions and technologies created or transformed whole industries, including the automobile, chemical, and airplane industries. Investment in both machinery and in workers' education raised worker productivity by a significant amount; the average worker produced two-thirds more in 1929 than in 1919. Workers' incomes increased by 23 percent, and corporate profits rose 62 percent. America's annual gross national product (GNP) reached heights never before attained in U.S. history; by 1929 it was 25 percent higher than the GNP of 1919. Such economic growth seemed a strong vindication of the policies and philosophy of the Republican presidents of the 1920s—Warren G. Harding and Calvin Coolidge. Their administrations were guided by the belief that the economy was essentially self-regulating, that downswings would correct themselves, that business leaders would ensure what was best for the nation, and that government should therefore not interfere in business matters.

One part of America's economy that received great attention in the 1920s was the booming stock market. One economic study calculated that if a person bought a representative group of stocks in 1921 and sold them in September 1929, the investor would have earned a return of 412 percent—excluding dividend payments. The rapidly rising prices encouraged many people to speculate in stocks, often with money borrowed from brokerages and banks. The rush of stock prices excited many Americans, although relatively few were directly involved in buying stocks. The stock market and news about it helped set America's optimistic mood. Historian William Leuchtenburg notes that

> even by the summer of 1929 the market had drawn people who never dreamed they would be caught in the speculative frenzy. How much longer could you hold out when your neighbor who bought General Motors at 99 in 1925 sold it at 212 in 1928. There were stories of a plunger who entered the market with a million dollars and ran it up to thirty millions in eight months, of a peddler who parlayed $4,000 into $250,000. The Bull Market was not simply a phenomenon of New York and Chicago; there were brokerage offices in towns like Steubenville, Ohio and Storm Lake, Iowa. Even non-investors followed the market news; like batting averages, it touched the statistical heart of the country.[1]

Many observers believed that the stock market boom and the generally good economic news of the 1920s foreshadowed an even brighter future. The United States had entered a new industrial era and had discovered a formula for permanent growth. "We are approaching equality of prosperity more rapidly than most people realize,"[2] wrote Harvard economist Thomas N. Carver in 1925. His optimism was shared by many, including President Herbert Hoover, who, upon taking the oath of office in March 1929, pledged to abolish poverty in the United States and declared that he had "no fears for the future of the country."

The Stock Market Crash and the End of Hope

Such hopes were to be cruelly dashed by the stock market crash of October 1929 and the economic crisis that followed—a crisis that lasted more than a decade and came to be known in history as the Great Depression. In some respects the story of the Great Depression goes beyond the depressed stock prices, high unemployment rates, and other economic statistics. The story of the Great Depression is one of destroyed hopes for the future for many Americans—as illustrated by the fact there were 250,000 fewer marriages in 1932 than in 1929. It is also a story of how Americans struggled to regain their faith in American institutions and how America's leaders, most notably Presidents Herbert Hoover and Franklin D. Roosevelt, sought to raise the collective hopes of all Americans that the Depression could end and that Americans could improve their lives.

The stock market crash was the first blow to the exuberance of the 1920s. By 1929 about 2 million Americans were investors in American securities, and the stock market hit record highs in September. In October, however, a flood of "sell" orders deluged Wall Street, dropping the value of stocks listed on the New York Stock Exchange $26 billion within a month. The market held brief rallies after that, but it generally continued to decline until July 1932—and even after that would recover very slowly. The value of General Motors stock, for example, fell from a high of more than $200 to a low of $8 in 1932.

The crash wiped out the savings of many investors and dried up funds for business investment. It also had a crucial psychological impact as people's belief in ever-expanding prosperity vanished and confidence in the economy waned. People suddenly cut back on purchases of new cars, appliances, and houses—which in turn depressed the American economy even more. The hopefulness that had buoyed American spirits and the American economy during the 1920s reversed in the 1930s. Business executives, spooked by the stock market collapse and declining sales, concluded that things were *not* going to improve anytime soon; they stopped making new investments in machinery, offices, and employees.

Signs of economic collapse were everywhere in the months and years following the crash. Manufacturers closed plants and laid off one hundred thousand workers a week. National unemployment steadily rose to over 20 percent—50 percent among black Americans. In some industrial centers such as Toledo, Ohio, the unemployment figure reached 80 percent. The unemployment deflated the general spirit and morale of the American people. Many contemporary observers and historians have observed the numbing effects of joblessness, especially among Americans raised to believe in self-sufficiency, providing for your own family, and making the best of your opportunities. Historian Ray Allen Billington, drawing on his own experiences of living through the Great Depression, recalled seeing unemployed workers and "their bleak downcast eyes, their broken spirit," and how "people seem to blame themselves."[3] Suicides of people who had lost jobs were common; some newspapers actually ran cartoons on the phenomenon. The suicide rate rose 25 percent between 1929 and 1933.

Hoover's Response

The president of the United States at the time of the Great Crash, Herbert Hoover, was a mining engineer and a self-made millionaire who, many Americans believed, embodied the best of the American dream. Historian Louis W. Liebovich writes that Hoover was "the boy who rose from humble beginnings to become a successful businessman through independence, hard work, and determination."[4] His administrative abilities were revealed in his efforts providing food relief to Europeans after World War I and by his record as secretary of commerce under two presidents in the 1920s. In some respects he seemed ideally placed to lead America in the trying economic times.

Hoover saw his role as president as being an "influential advisor and well-placed cheerleader."[5] He brought together business, local government, and labor leaders and exhorted them to take unselfish steps to maintain wages, desist from strikes or layoffs, and continue investing in companies and public works. He made a series of speeches to the American people urging them not to let the stock market crash panic them (to this end, he avoided use of the word *panic* to describe the state of the American economy and pioneered the use of the term *depression* instead, implying that what was happening was just a small obstacle on the normally smooth road of economic progress). The "fundamental business of the country," he spoke shortly after the stock market crash, "is on a sound and prosperous basis." He later declared that the country needed a "big laugh" to help people "forget their troubles and the depression."[6] As long as people believed in the future and bought and invested the same as they did in the 1920s, the collapse would be short-lived.

Unfortunately for Hoover and the nation, his hopeful predictions, repeated time and time again, failed to be self-fulfilling. Part of Hoover's problem was personality; he often appeared stiff and formal in his public appearances. In addition, Hoover often seemed incapable of fully grasping the size of the economic difficulties facing Americans and woefully out of touch with their troubles. "Many persons have left their jobs for the more profitable one of selling apples," he once stated. On another occasion he spoke of "hoboes [who] are better fed than they have ever been. One hobo in New York got ten meals in one day."[7]

Hoover's actions and speeches also seemed of little help to the many Americans who had missed out on the prosperity during the 1920s and who faced even more dire circumstances in the 1930s. The prosperity of the 1920s had been far from equally distributed among all Americans. Forty percent of all families in 1929 had incomes under fifteen hundred dollars—and America's twenty-four thousand richest families had incomes three times as large as that of the almost 6 million poorest families. Farmers had seen their incomes fall by nearly 50 percent in the 1920s as prices for their products fell. Workers in several industries, including textiles and coal mining, had suffered from chronic unemployment.

These people as well as others who were victimized by the Great Depression believed that Hoover would act to support big banks and big businesses but not the average American. This suspicion was grounded in fact. Hoover went further than all of his presidential predecessors in enlisting the federal government to help businesses (on the theory that by helping businesses he could help put people back to work). However, he consistently maintained that providing direct relief to individuals threatened by penury and hunger by events of the Great Depression was not the proper responsibility of the federal government but rather of private charities and local communities. He stated his reasons in a 1931 speech:

This is not an issue as to whether people shall go hungry or cold in the United States. It is solely a question of the best method by which hunger and cold shall be prevented. It is a question as to whether the American people on one hand will maintain the spirit of charity and mutual self help through voluntary giving and the responsibility of local government as distinguished on the other hand from appropriations out of the Federal Treasury for such purposes. My own conviction is strongly that if we break down this sense of responsibility of individual generosity to individual and mutual self help in the country in times of national difficulty and if we start appropriations of this character we have not only impaired something infinitely valuable in the life of the American people but have struck at the roots of self-government. Once this has happened it is not the cost of the few score millions but we are faced with the abyss of reliance in future upon Government charity in some form or other. The money involved is indeed the least of the costs to American ideals and American institutions.[8]

It is important to remember that Hoover's beliefs regarding the role of government were not unusual but were the orthodox wisdom of the time. But by 1932 Hoover was being widely and personally blamed for the continuing economic distress. Shantytowns on the outskirts of cities where homeless people lived were called "Hoovervilles," and newspapers wrapped around the body for warmth became "Hoover blankets."

The Socialist Alternative

For a minority of Americans, hope in ending the Great Depression lay only in the prospect of radical changes in America's economic and political system—one that specifically excluded the big businesses and capitalists that Hoover and others believed were the foundation of American prosperity in the 1920s. In September 1932 the journal *New Masses* published a symposium in which notable intellectuals, including Upton Sinclair and Edmund Wilson, declared that socialism alone could save the country. The Socialist Party platform stated that "we are facing a breakdown of the capitalistic system. . . .The capitalistic system is now creaking and breaking in every joint."[9]

On the other side of the world, the Soviet Union had created an entirely different system—one in which private property had been eliminated and the economy and government were managed by the Communist Party for (presumably) all the workers. While the United States, by then the world's preeminent capitalist country, was struggling, the Soviet Union had a system in which five-year plans determined what was to be produced in order to meet the people's actual needs, unencumbered by frivolous waste and a parasitic capitalist class of employers. Historian Richard H. Pells writes that for some Americans, the Soviet Union's "thriving five-year plans and its sure sense of direction seemed somehow a reproach to confused, tired, chaotic America."[10] Many Americans visited Russia to be shown the country's achievements; others joined Marxist and Socialist political organizations. Although few were active Communists who sought a similar revolution in America, many concluded that America could draw lessons from the Soviet experience concerning greater central planning for the economy. Stuart Chase, the author of several popular books on economics and government, wrote in a 1931 book that, "for Russians, the world is exciting, stimulating, challenging, calling forth their interest and enthusiasm. The world for most Americans is dull and uninteresting, wracked with frightful economic insecurity."[11]

The Socialist candidate for president received 880,000 votes in 1932—the party's best showing since 1920. However, most Americans went with another alternative to Herbert Hoover.

Franklin D. Roosevelt

Hoover's opponent in the 1932 election was Franklin D. Roosevelt, a distant cousin of former president Theodore Roosevelt. Roosevelt was a rising political star in the Democratic Party (he was its vice-presidential nominee in 1920) when, in 1921, he was stricken by polio, which left him paralyzed from the waist down (a condition that was never really illustrated in the many political cartoons drawn about him). Many historians and contemporary observers believe that Roosevelt's experience with polio helped to transform him and prepare him to lead the nation through the Great Depression. Frances Perkins, who served as Roosevelt's secretary of labor during his terms as New York governor and as president, later argued that

> Franklin Roosevelt underwent a spiritual transformation during the years of his illness. I noticed that when he came back that the years of pain and suffering had purged that slightly arrogant attitude he had displayed on occasion before he was stricken. . . . Having been to the depths of trouble, he understood the problems of people in trouble.[12]

When the Great Depression hit America in 1929, Roosevelt was serving as governor of the state of New York. He battled a Republican-dominated state legislature for several progressive reforms, including legislation proposing an eight-hour workday and five-day workweek. In 1931 he became the first governor to set up an effective state relief program. In an address to the state legislature, he expressed his belief that the government should assume responsibility for helping people in need: "I assert that modern society, acting through its government, owes the definite obligation to prevent the starvation or dire want of any of its fellow men and women who try to maintain themselves but cannot."[13]

Roosevelt's actions in New York attracted nationwide attention, and he was selected as the Democratic Party's presidential nominee in July 1932. In the fall campaign he spoke of the "forgotten man" and of a "new deal" for the American people, but he was vague about the details. The election of 1932 was, if not necessarily a sweeping victory for Roosevelt, a sweeping repudiation of Hoover and the Republican Party. Democrats gained large majorities in both houses of Congress for the first time since the Civil War. Roosevelt won the electoral vote in all but five northeastern states and became the first Democrat to win a majority of the nation's popular vote since Franklin Pierce in 1852.

Restoring America's Confidence

Like Hoover before him, one of Roosevelt's primary goals was the restoration of hope and confidence in the nation's future. Thus, in his inaugural address on March 4, 1933, Roosevelt spoke these famous words: "This great nation will endure as it has endured, will revive and will prosper. So first of all, let me assert my firm belief that the only thing we have to fear is fear itself—nameless, unreasoning, unjustified terror which paralyzes needed efforts to convert retreat into advance."[14] This did not mean refusing to acknowledge the realities of the Great Depression, as critics believed Hoover had done. Roosevelt stated in the same speech:

> The withered leaves of industrial enterprise lie on every side; farmers find no markets for their produce; the savings of many years in thousands of families are gone. More important, a host of unemployed citizens face the grim problem of

existence, and an equally great number toil with little return. Only a foolish optimist can deny the dark realities of the moment.[15]

To meet this crisis, Roosevelt pledged action and argued that, if necessary, he would "ask Congress for the one remaining instrument to meet the crisis—broad Executive power to wage a war against the emergency, as great as the power that would be given to me if we were in fact invaded by a foreign foe."[16] Congress responded to Roosevelt's plea by supporting a wide variety of programs during his first term, creating what some called an "alphabet soup" of new federal government programs and agencies.

Relief, Recovery, and Reform

Roosevelt embraced government action far more than his predecessor to address what he called the three Rs: relief, recovery, and reform. For relief of the unemployed, the hungry, and people in danger of losing their homes, Congress and Roosevelt enacted a variety of programs and agencies between 1933 and 1935. The Civilian Conservation Corps employed young men in conservation and reforestation projects. The Federal Emergency Relief Administration and Civil Works Administration spent $2 billion in welfare and work relief programs between 1933 and 1935. The Home Owners Loan Corporation prevented thousands of property owners from having their homes and other assets foreclosed. The Works Progress Administration, created in 1935, oversaw numerous public employment projects over its eight-year history, creating thousands of hospitals, schools, and parks, and providing financial aid for artists, writers, and students.

The key New Deal programs to promote economic recovery were the National Recovery Administration (NRA) and the Agricultural Adjustment Administration (AAA). The NRA attempted to impose some degree of planning on the nation's businesses by encouraging them to establish codes setting standards on production, wages, and prices. The AAA sought to raise depressed farm prices by encouraging farmers to produce fewer crops. Both programs had some initial success in their professed goals of stabilizing prices; both were also criticized by some for catering to big businesses and commercial farmers at the expense of small businesses, small and tenant farmers, and workers. The Supreme Court later found parts of the legislation creating the NRA and the AAA to be unconstitutional.

The New Deal also enacted several important and lasting laws aimed to reform economic and business institutions that many believed had failed America in the Great Depression. The Federal Deposit Insurance Corporation was created to reorganize the nation's bank system and prevent future bank panics and failures. The Banking Act of 1935 empowered the Federal Reserve Board to set interest rates, increasing the federal government's control over the nation's monetary policy. The Securities and Exchange Commission was created to regulate stock exchanges and restore public confidence in investing. Other laws ensured the rights of workers to bargain collectively in labor unions and set some standards on working hours and conditions.

Perhaps the most important New Deal accomplishment was the Social Security Act of 1935, which combined elements of all three Rs. It involved the federal government in establishing a system of old-age pensions, unemployment insurance, and welfare benefits for needy disabled persons and dependent children.

Contemporary observers and historians generally agree that the New Deal did not have a coherent underlying plan or philosophy. Some of the initiatives seemed to work at cross-purposes with each other. Roosevelt continued to criticize federal deficit spending and cut wages for federal government employees even as New Deal programs hired new workers. Efforts to raise farm prices through the AAA resulted in harder times for people struggling to pay more for food. Efforts by public work relief projects to stimulate the economy were hampered by the fact that they only hired a fraction of the nation's unemployed and generally paid very low wages. What made it all work, many believe, was Roosevelt himself. Speaking to the nation directly in numerous radio "fireside chats," press conferences, and speeches, the president projected a warm personality and proved more able than his predecessor in inspiring public confidence and hope for the future.

What Did the New Deal Achieve?

John T. Flynn, a journalist during the Roosevelt era, later asserted that the New Deal had no real effect on the Great Depression:

In his first two full terms of eight years, President Roosevelt never produced any recovery whatever. When he was elected there were 11,586,000 persons unemployed. In 1939— seven years later—when the war struck in Europe, there were still 11,369,000 persons unemployed. . . . In 1932 when he was elected there were 4,155,000 households with 16,620,000 persons on relief. In 1939, seven years later, there were 4,227,000 households with 19,648,000 persons on relief. In the presence of these undisputed facts how can any sober-minded citizen suppose that Mr. Roosevelt brought recovery to the United States.[17]

Many modern historians agree with Flynn. As historian Alan Brinkley puts it, Roosevelt's New Deal did not "end the Great Depression and the massive unemployment that accompanied it; only the enormous public and private spending for World War II finally did that."[18] Brinkley goes on to assert that the New Deal

did not, the complaints of conservative critics, notwithstanding, transform American capitalism in any radical way; except in the field of labor relations, corporate power remained nearly as free from government regulation or control in 1945 as it had been in 1933. The New Deal did not end poverty or effect any significant redistribution of wealth.[19]

However, the New Deal did have substantial achievements and legacies. It committed the federal government to provide at least some protection for the poor and unemployed, help protect labor unions, regulate and stabilize banking and the stock markets, provide low-income housing, and other areas previously outside its purview. Government before the New Deal had often served only the needs of business interests; under the New Deal farmers, workers, consumers, and others could press their demands upon the government. Historian Samuel Eliot Morison wrote that the New Deal "gave the ordinary citizen a feeling of financial security against old age, sickness, and unemployment which he had never enjoyed, and a participation in government such as he had never seen since Lincoln's era."[20]

Perhaps most important, and the factor that perhaps most accounts for the political realignment that left the Democratic Party the majority party for more than a generation after the Great

Depression ended, was that Franklin D. Roosevelt was able to instill in Americans some sense of hope in their nation's economic and political system, whose survival had been in danger during the Great Depression. When Roosevelt became president, George Wolfskill and John A. Hudson write, the American people had experienced "a unity of erosion, an erosion of intangibles, of will, of pride, of self-respect, of confidence. . . . It was an erosion measured in the melting away of life savings, in the foreclosing of mortgages, . . . selling precious household belongings. . . , in the shame . . . of honest men asking for relief." They argue that perhaps the greatest achievement of Roosevelt's New Deal was to halt this erosion of hope—in a sense stalling for time—"time for the people to pull themselves together, shake their fears, recover their sense of humor, take heart. Time so that America would not default to madmen and lunatics and their wicked dreams. Time so that honest men could find solid answers to pressing problems that the country had been ignoring and fending off for years."[21]

As the generation of Americans that lived through the Great Depression slowly passes from the scene, it is up to future generations to remember the crisis it faced in the Great Depression and to study how America responded to and survived it. Among the most evocative responses to the Great Depression are to be found in the efforts of the nation's political cartoonists. The works in this volume reveal how Americans responded to the crisis of hope that was the Great Depression.

Notes

1. Quoted in Thomas E. Hall and J. Davidson Ferguson, *The Great Depression: An International Disaster of Perverse Economic Policies.* Lansing: University of Michigan, 1998.

2. Quoted in Irwin Unger, *These United States: The Questions of Our Past.* Englewood Cliffs, NJ: Prentice Hall, 1989, p. 674.

3. Quoted in Robert Kelley, *The Shaping of the American Past*, 5th ed., Englewood Cliffs, NJ: Prentice Hall, 1990, p. 599.

4. Louis W. Liebovich, *Bylines in Despair: Herbert Hoover, the Great Depression, and the U.S. News Media.* Westport, CT: Praeger, 1994, p. xiii.

5. Quoted in Kelley, *The Shaping of the American Past*, p. 596.

6. Quoted in Unger, *These United States: The Questions of Our Past*, p. 709.

7. Quoted in Winthrop Jordan et al., *The United States*, 6th ed., Englewood Cliffs, NJ: Prentice Hall, 1987, p. 633.

8. Quoted in William S. Myers and Walter H. Newton, *The Hoover Administration: A Documented Narrative*. New York: Charles Scribner's Sons, 1936, pp. 63–64.

9. Quoted in Don Nardo, ed., *The Great Depression*. San Diego: Greenhaven Press, 2000, p. 38.

10. Quoted in Kelley, *The Shaping of the American Past*, p. 609.

11. Quoted in Kelley, *The Shaping of the American Past*, pp. 609–10.

12. Quoted in Nathan Miller, *F.D.R.: An Intimate History*. New York: Meridian, 1984, p. 197.

13. Quoted in Ted Morgan, *FDR: A Biography*. New York: Simon and Schuster, 1985, p. 321.

14. Quoted in Richard Hofstadter, *Great Issues in American History: From Reconstruction to the Present Day*. New York: Vintage Books, 1982, p. 344.

15. Quoted in Hofstadter, *Great Issues in American History*, p. 344.

16. Quoted in Hofstadter, *Great Issues in American History*, pp. 348–49.

17. John T. Flynn, *The Roosevelt Myth*. New York: Devin-Adair, 1956, p. 46.

18. Alan Brinkley, "The New Deal: An Overview," *Social Education*, September 1996.

19. Brinkley, "The New Deal."

20. Quoted in Bryan J. Grapes, *Franklin D. Roosevelt*. San Diego: Greenhaven Press, 2001, p. 31.

21. George Wolfskill and John A. Hudson, *All but the People: Franklin D. Roosevelt and His Critics, 1933–1939*. New York: Scribner, 1969.

Chapter 1

The Depression Sets In

Preface

The Great Depression caused serious personal hardships for millions of Americans. People from different walks of life were affected by the Great Depression in different ways, but all were affected to some degree by the economic disaster.

The first people to be hit hard were those involved in the stock market, including investors and people connected with stock market firms. The stock market crash of October 1929 decimated the fortunes of investors, many of whom had borrowed money to invest in stocks. The slide in stock market values continued through July 1932, by which time $70 billion in investments had been erased.

The effects of the stock market crash soon reached even those Americans who had resisted the urge to speculate in stocks. America's banking structure crumbled as people who had borrowed money to invest in the stock market could not repay their loans and nervous customers sought to withdraw their money. Banks cut credit to businesses and foreign borrowers, thus cramping both business investment and foreign trade. Between the stock market crash and the end of President Herbert Hoover's term in March 1933, more than nine thousand U.S. banks failed and closed their doors—including four thousand in the first two months in 1933 alone. Each bank failure represented the loss of the life savings of its customers.

The stock market crash also contributed to a cycle that affected American consumers and workers. Much of the prosperity of the 1920s was the result of spending by American families on such products as cars, radios, appliances, and other consumer goods. But because of the stock market crash, many Americans cut back on their consumption of such items. This frugality among consumers led retail stores to cut back their orders, and factories to pare back their production and investment. Ultimately workers at factories and stores were confronted with unemployment and/or lower wages, which reduced consumer spending further, leading to another cycle of economic decline. In 1930, 26,655 U.S. businesses failed, a record number that was eclipsed the following year when 28,285 went bankrupt. By 1932 the nation's volume of manufacturing was a little over half of its 1929 peak.

Unemployment, which stood at about 3 percent before October 1929, rose to 9 percent by early 1930 and continued to rise until a quarter of America's workforce was unemployed (for black Americans, the unemployment rate rose to nearly 50 percent). In this time before federal government welfare departments and social programs, many unemployed workers had few resources to cushion them. Private charities were overwhelmed. Three states and hundreds of municipalities went bankrupt trying to cope with widespread poverty and declining tax revenues. Families were evicted from homes. Many people became hoboes, traveling by freight train from place to place looking for work.

In addition to its impact on workers in cities, the Great Depression also affected rural America, where 30 percent of Americans still lived in 1934. Many farmers were already struggling even prior to the October 1929 crash due to debt, overproduction, and low prices for their crops. The ensuing economic difficulties of the Great Depression—as well as drought in some states that turned large agricultural areas into a "dust bowl"—only exacerbated their problems. Between 1930 and 1935 as many as 750,000 farmers lost their farms due to foreclosures.

From stockbrokers to farmers, Americans were impacted by the severe economic slowdown of the 1930s. The cartoons in this chapter depict some of the human ramifications of the Great Depression.

Examining Cartoon 1:
"Leaves Are Scattered but Tree Is Unchanged"

Leaves Are Scattered but Tree Is Unchanged

About the Cartoon

Although economists and historians continue to debate whether the 1929 stock market crash *caused* all the economic hardships that followed, most historians mark the crash as a starting point of the Great Depression. Stock prices in the United States reached an all-time high in early September 1929, but then began to drift downward. On October 21, 1929, stock prices on the New York Stock Exchange fell drastically and continued to tumble until October 29. On that "Black Tuesday," the most disastrous single day in the history of the exchange, 16 million shares were sold and billions of dollars in stock value vanished.

President Herbert Hoover had responded to the ongoing stock market decline by pronouncing on October 24 that "the fundamental business of the country . . . is on a sound and prosperous basis," and many economic experts shared this conviction. This cartoon, published on October 30, 1929, provides an optimistic view of the long-term effects of the stock market crash. The top panel depicts a group of speculative investors happily looking at the "paper profits" they have made buying stocks (many Americans had used borrowed money to play the market, a practice that itself drove up stock prices). The second panel shows both profits and speculators being blown away by a "stock-selling blast" wind, but the tree, representing "American industry," remains standing. The cartoon suggests that while the stock market crash ended the dreams of making easy money through stock speculation, it did not change the essential strength and productivity of American business.

About the Cartoonist

John T. McCutcheon began his career as a sketch artist and illustrator for the *Chicago Morning News* in 1889. He was the editorial cartoonist for the *Chicago Tribune* from 1913 to 1954 and was regarded as one of America's most influential cartoonists for much of his career. He won a Pulitzer Prize in 1932.

Examining Cartoon 2:
"Gee—! That's Swell!!"

"GEE—! THAT'S SWELL!!"

About the Cartoon

The 1929 stock market crash wiped out the net worth of many investors and set in motion economic events that culminated in the Great Depression. This cartoon was first published on October 27, 1929, when the U.S. stock market was in the middle of a steep decline, and presents a more pessimistic view of the stock market crash than the preceding cartoon. It depicts a poorly dressed "market victim" reading a newspaper (presumably scavenged from the garbage can) in which President Herbert Hoover is defending the general state of American business. The caption suggests that the person in the cartoon takes little comfort from Hoover's words.

About the Cartoonist

From 1924 to 1948 Edmund Duffy was the editorial cartoonist for the *Baltimore Sun*, where he developed a national reputation and won three Pulitzer Prizes. He subsequently worked for the *Saturday Evening Post*.

Examining Cartoon 3:
"Direct Relief in Missouri"

About the Cartoon

This cartoon gives a picture of the dire straits faced by many families during the Great Depression. It shows a mother of two children sitting on a box, her head resting in despair on the table, and the father entering the door, presumably returning from an unsuccessful search for work. His face is drawn as a skull with its features spelling out "45 cents a day"—the amount that the state of Missouri then provided to needy families.

About the Cartoonist

Daniel Fitzpatrick was the editorial cartoonist for the *St. Louis Post-Dispatch* for forty-five years, during which time he drew fourteen thousand cartoons. His work, noted for its dark and somber style of drawing, won Pulitzer Prizes in 1926 and 1955.

Examining Cartoon 4:
"A Wise Economist Asks a Question"

About the Cartoon

One especially devastating aspect of the Great Depression was the wave of bank failures it caused. Between January 1930 and March 1933, more than nine thousand banks in the United States failed, wiping out the savings of millions of people who had thought that their money was secure. The cartoon shows a respectable middle-class man discussing his situation with a squirrel (an animal who presumably knows about saving for harder times). The man is revealed as someone who was neither lazy nor profligate, but a victim of forces that were outside his control. This cartoon won its creator, John T. McCutcheon, a Pulitzer Prize in 1932.

About the Cartoonist

John T. McCutcheon began his career as a sketch artist and illustrator for the *Chicago Morning News* in 1889. He was the editorial cartoonist for the *Chicago Tribune* from 1913 to 1954, and was regarded as one of America's most influential cartoonists for much of his career. Much of his popularity stemmed from his political and human interest cartoons that celebrated the values and rhythms of rural Midwestern life.

Chapter 2

President Hoover Responds

EXAMINING ISSUES THROUGH
POLITICAL CARTOONS

Preface

The early years of the Great Depression are inseparably linked to the presidency of Herbert Hoover. Ironically, when Hoover won forty out of forty-eight states in a sweeping election victory to be president of the United States in 1928, he seemed a perfect match for what Americans anticipated as a "new era" of prosperity and technological progress. Hoover, a mining engineer, self-made millionaire, and well-regarded secretary of commerce under Presidents Warren G. Harding and Calvin Coolidge, seemed to epitomize the American dream of success. In his inaugural address, delivered in March 1929, he optimistically pledged to abolish poverty in America.

Less than nine months later the stock market endured several brutal days that became known as the Great Crash. Although historians presently dispute how much the stock market crash is to blame for what followed, the economy went into sharp decline for the rest of Hoover's term in office. Consumer spending fell from $203.6 billion in 1929 to $141.5 billion in 1933. Business investment fell from $40.4 billion to $5.3 billion. Unemployment rose from 3.2 percent to 24.9 percent.

Hoover's response to the Depression was shaped by his belief that it was not the federal government's job to provide "government charity" to individuals in need. He saw himself, in the months following the 1929 crash, as limited to being an "influential advisor and well-placed cheerleader." He held conferences with business leaders and urged them to work together to not lay off workers or lower wages. He urged labor leaders to desist from strikes, bankers to cooperate with each other to prevent weaker banks from failing, and local governments to provide relief and public works. His exhortations, without the force of law, mostly failed to achieve their desired goals. His efforts as a cheerleader, which consisted mainly of periodic predictions that recovery was just around the corner and statements such as, "What this country needs is a good big laugh," failed to boost American morale.

As the Depression continued to worsen, Hoover began to propose more drastic government actions. In 1931 he offered government help to the economy in the form of the Reconstruction Finance Corporation (RFC). The RFC would lend money to faltering banks and businesses in order to stimulate economic activity and restore public confidence in the economy. Enacted in January 1932, it loaned more than $1 billion to businesses in its first year. Despite these and other programs that provided aid to businesses, Hoover continued to refuse on principle to grant federal money directly to the nation's poor and unemployed. Hoover was not alone in opposing federal aid; many economists opposed even Hoover's limited government measures to assist businesses.

By 1932 America was in dire straits; 273,000 families were evicted from their homes that year alone. Thousands of banks had gone under, leaving many people without their life savings. Historian Richard H. Pells writes that many Americans were simply demoralized. "The depression meant more than simply the failure of business; it was to many people an overwhelming natural catastrophe." Although Hoover had done more than any previous U.S. president to use government resources to fix the economy, by 1932 he had become identified with the Great Depression in the public's mind. Shantytowns housing homeless and jobless people became known as "Hoovervilles," and "Hoover flags" were pockets turned inside out to indicate penury. Hoover was booed everywhere he campaigned in the 1932 presidential election against Democratic candidate Franklin D. Roosevelt; he was defeated by a greater margin than his own landslide victory in 1928. The American people looked to a new president to lead the nation out of the Great Depression.

Examining Cartoon 1:

"Got an Extra One of Them Moratoriums, Mister?"

"Got an Extra One of Them Moratoriums, Mister?"

About the Cartoon

By 1931 it was clear that President Hoover's initial steps to help America's economy—which included private talks with business and labor leaders, optimistic statements to the public, some federal funding of construction programs, and calls on state and local governments to increase public-works projects—were insufficient. Hoover's next major initiatives focused on the international economy, which he believed was a primary cause of America's problems. The growing difficulties European nations had in paying back debts to the United States incurred during World War I had created an international banking crisis. In July 1931 Hoover announced a one-year moratorium on payment of debts that foreign nations owed to the U.S. government.

Hoover's announcement was praised by many as a sensible contribution to international goodwill and recovery. But others contended that the moratorium mainly benefited bankers and holders of foreign bonds at a time when many Americans, including America's farmers, faced crushing debts and mortgages of their own. In addition to debt, many of America's farms were in crisis because of bad weather and low crop prices. This cartoon by Edmund Duffy responds to Hoover's announcement of a foreign debt moratorium by criticizing the president's failure to make a similar gesture to America's farmers.

About the Cartoonist

From 1924 to 1948, Edmund Duffy was the editorial cartoonist for the *Baltimore Sun*, where he developed a national reputation and won three Pulitzer Prizes. He subsequently worked for the *Saturday Evening Post*.

Examining Cartoon 2:
"The Skipper Sights Land Again"

THE SKIPPER SIGHTS LAND AGAIN

About the Cartoon

On August 26, 1932, President Herbert Hoover announced that the "major financial crisis" facing the United States was over. This was not the first time the president had made such an optimistic prediction about the state of the economy, however. Cartoonist Rollin Kirby expresses his skepticism about Hoover's claim in this August 29 cartoon in which Hoover is cast as Noah from the biblical story of the great flood. Hoover is announcing that he has successfully spotted land (according to tradition, the mountaintop on which the ark finally came to rest is Mount Ararat). An elephant, the traditional symbol of the Republican Party, is looking on with interest, perhaps a reflection of the fact that the Republican Party's political fortunes sorely depended on some economic good news. No land is actually seen in the cartoon, and its caption suggests that this was not the first such announcement—and perhaps not the last, either. Kirby implies there is no such end in sight for the "flood" of joblessness, bank failures, and other economic travails facing America despite Hoover's predictions to the contrary.

About the Cartoonist

Rollin Kirby began his illustrating and cartooning career in 1901, when he began drawing pictures for leading magazines including *Collier's*, *McClure's*, *Life*, and *Harper's*. From 1913 to 1931, Rollin Kirby was an editorial cartoonist for the *New York World,* one of the nation's leading liberal publications. His cartoons attacking prohibitionists and conservative politicians and championing such causes as woman's suffrage and the New Deal made him widely known. In 1922 Kirby won the first-ever Pulitzer Prize in the cartoonist category; he also took the prize in 1924 and 1929. After the *World* folded in 1931, Kirby continued as political cartoonist for the *World-Telegram* until he resigned in March 1939 because of disagreements with that publication's conservative political positions.

Examining Cartoon 3:

"We'd Have Found Out If We Hadn't Had 'Em."

We'd have found out if we hadn't had 'em.

About the Cartoon

This cartoon by Jay Norwood ("Ding") Darling was first published on October 17, 1932, shortly before the 1932 presidential election, in which President Herbert Hoover was being challenged by New York governor Franklin D. Roosevelt. Darling, a consistent supporter of Hoover, makes a case for the president in the cartoon by answering the question (posed by a person representing the Democratic Party) about what good Hoover's programs have been. The cartoon answers the question by depicting various Hoover programs and initiatives as valuable parachutes that have enabled America's farmers, homeowners, workers, and others to survive the economic hard times much better than people in other countries. The cartoonist does not contend that Hoover's initiatives and programs have actually revived the economy and ended the Great Depression. But Hoover's programs, Darling argues, have prevented conditions from getting even worse. Among the specific programs he defends in this panel are the Reconstruction Finance Corporation, a government program created in January 1932 to provide loans to businesses, the creation of twelve Federal Home Loan Banks to provide funds for residences and farms, and federal programs to provide farmers with money to buy seeds.

About the Cartoonist

Jay Norwood Darling, who signed his cartoons as "Ding," drew more than seventeen thousand cartoons for the *Des Moines (Iowa) Register* during a long career that spanned from 1906 to 1949. Beginning in 1917, his work was also published in the *New York Tribune* and nationally syndicated, making Darling one of the nation's foremost cartoonists of his time. He was a strong admirer of Herbert Hoover and later became a personal friend of the president. Darling received the Pulitzer Prize for cartoons in 1924 and 1943.

Chapter 3

Business Versus Labor in the Great Depression

Preface

L abor unions and (sometimes violent) labor strikes had been a part of American economic history long before the onset of the Great Depression in 1929. However, the Great Depression marked the revival and expansion of the American labor movement both in terms of government recognition of labor rights and a new wave of strikes and other acts of worker militancy.

During the 1920s employers had successfully managed to mostly avoid dealing with unions. Workers were required to sign "yellow-dog" contracts agreeing never to join a union. Firms refused to do business with companies that hired union labor. State manufacturers' associations made pacts in which they agreed never to negotiate with a union. Employers were aided in their antiunion efforts by state and local governments. Courts issued injunctions forbidding strikes and union organizing, and local police and the National Guard were frequently called on to forcibly put down strikes. By 1932 only about one in ten workers belonged to a labor union.

During the Great Depression several laws were passed that changed the status of labor unions. The 1932 Norris–La Guardia Anti-Injunction Act outlawed yellow-dog contracts and forbade federal courts from issuing injunctions against strikes and other collective bargaining practices. Section 7A of the National Industrial Recovery Act, a 1933 law that was one of the first New Deal laws passed, affirmed the right of labor to bargain collectively and set up a national labor board to handle labor disputes. When that legislation was invalidated by the Supreme Court in 1935, Congress passed the National Labor Relations Act in 1935. That law reaffirmed the right of workers to organize and created the more powerful National Labor Relations Board (NLRB), a federal agency that was given the power to *order* employers to bargain with the unions that represented the majority of their workers (as determined by worker elections supervised by the NLRB).

The increased government backing helped to grow union membership dramatically, from 2.6 million in 1933 to 8.7 million in 1939 (28.6 percent of the nonfarm labor force). Much of the growth in labor unions took place among unskilled workers in the great mass-production industries, including auto, rubber, and steel. This era also witnessed a new burst of strikes—strikes that were often accompanied by violence as strikers clashed with police, vigilantes hired by companies, replacement workers, and in some cases rival unions. In 1933 fifteen strikers were killed on picket lines; the next year forty were killed. In January 1936 workers unveiled a new tactic —the sit-down strike, in which strikers remained inside factories and prevented them from being operated by replacement workers. Although many Americans sympathized with workers and their demands, others blamed unions for strikes and the violence and economic disruption surrounding them. The following cartoons capture some of the public reaction to the labor strife of the Great Depression.

Examining Cartoon 1:
"Is This Recovery?"

About the Cartoon

In 1934 alone, roughly 1.5 million workers went on strike seeking higher wages and better working conditions. The cartoon, drawn when dockworkers in San Francisco and truckers in Minnesota, among other groups, were on strike, questions whether such actions might impede America's economic recovery. It shows Uncle Sam attempting to enter a door marked "The Way Out of the Depression," only to be barred by a worker leaning the other way.

About the Cartoonist

Lute Pease, a former ranch hand in California and gold miner in Alaska, worked as a political cartoonist and correspondent for several West Coast publications before joining the *Newark* (New Jersey) *Evening News* as its political cartoonist in 1914. He was still with the *Evening News* when he won the 1949 Pulitzer Prize for cartooning at the age of eighty.

Examining Cartoon 2:
"Strike-Breaking"

About the Cartoon

From 1933 to 1941, union membership rose from under 3 million to more than 8 million. But the efforts by unions to enroll members and strike for better wages and working conditions were staunchly resisted by many employers and businesses. Steel executive Tom Girdler, automaker Henry Ford, and other employers used spies, strikebreakers, legal injunctions, and in some cases violence and intimidation to break strikes and discourage union activity. The cartoon depicts a worker being victimized by union-breaking thugs. The cartoon also belittles government and law enforcement agencies with its portrayal of an ineffectual "fact-finding" investigator.

About the Cartoonist

William Gropper, born to a poor Jewish immigrant family in New York, was a noted cartoonist and painter whose work championed working-class concerns. After his radical political beliefs (and the revelation that he had contributed anonymous drawings to the Communist newspaper *Daily Worker*) led to his dismissal from his first cartoonist job at the *New York Herald Tribune*, Gropper contributed work to a wide variety of publications ranging from the *New Masses* to *Vanity Fair*. His paintings are now featured in many museums and collections.

Examining Cartoon 3:

"Sure, I'll Work for Both Sides"

About the Cartoon

The year 1934 was marked by several bitter and violent strikes. In Minnesota, clashes between workers and police in May left four dead and two hundred wounded. Also in that year, striking dock workers on the West Coast, including workers in San Francisco and Seattle, clashed with company and law enforcement officials during a long struggle to obtain union recognition. This cartoon, first published in September 1934, personifies violence as a towering, menacing figure armed with bricks and bombs straddling a fence between industry and workers. The cartoonist suggests that neither side will ultimately benefit from violent tactics.

About the Cartoonist

Ross A. Lewis, a former commercial artist, was hired as the *Milwaukee Journal*'s political cartoonist in 1932. He won the 1935 Pulitzer Prize for cartooning.

Chapter 4

Roosevelt's New Deal

Preface

W hen New York governor Franklin D. Roosevelt broke political precedent by flying to Chicago to accept the Democratic presidential nomination in person, he pledged "a new deal for the American people." With no end in sight to the Great Depression, Roosevelt went on to defeat incumbent president Herbert Hoover in the November presidential election in 1932. (Roosevelt would win reelection in 1936, 1940, and 1944.) The phrase *New Deal* has become the label of Roosevelt's domestic program in his first two terms of office, during which he went much further than Hoover had in enlisting the federal government to promote economic recovery and deliver relief to the American people. Historian Alan Brinkley writes, "The New Deal consisted of many different efforts to end the Great Depression and reform the American economy. Most of them failed, but there were enough successes to establish it as the most important episode of the twentieth century in the creation of the modern American state."

Brinkley and other historians have divided the New Deal into several distinct phases. The first phase took place during the first weeks and months after Roosevelt was inaugurated as president in March 1933—a time when the Great Depression was at its worst. Public desperation and the election of many Democrats to Congress in the 1932 elections enabled Roosevelt to propose and enact numerous initiatives during the first hundred days of his administration. One of Roosevelt's first acts was to declare a banking holiday and pass legislation to restore public confidence in the nation's banking system. The passage of the Emergency Banking Act was followed in subsequent weeks by a flurry of other laws and programs. These included the Agricultural Adjustment Act (AAA), a federal program of subsidies and production controls for American farmers; the creation of the Securities and Exchange Commission to oversee and restore confidence in the stock market; and the creation of the Civilian Conservation Corps, a federal program that put millions of unemployed Americans in government jobs to work in public lands. Another important piece of New Deal legislation was the National Industrial Recovery Act (NIRA), which attempted to stabilize prices and wages through cooperative "codes" agreed to by businesses and labor leaders. In this and other acts, Roosevelt attempted to unite business and labor interests in promoting economic recovery.

The second phase of the New Deal was a series of laws passed in 1935. By this time the New Deal's initial laws had created broad popular support for Roosevelt's administration, had provided some measure of relief for the unemployed, and were also credited with restoring public confidence in the nation's banks. However, America's economy was still in a depressed state compared to pre-1929 levels, and Roosevelt and his New Deal were under attack from several different directions. The Supreme Court struck down several key New Deal laws, including NIRA and the AAA, on the grounds that they exceeded the federal government's constitutional powers to control the economy. Meanwhile, many business leaders and wealthy Americans were becoming increasingly critical of what they viewed as the dangerously socialistic nature of Roosevelt's reforms. In 1934, for example, a group of conservative political and business leaders formed the American Liberty League, which published and distributed pamphlets attacking the New Deal as un-American and unconstitutional.

Roosevelt also received much criticism from the other side of the political spectrum for not going far enough in altering America's political and economic system. Three strikingly different personalities gained national prominence as New Deal critics. Charles Coughlin was a controversial Roman Catholic priest whose radio-broadcast sermons included political passages that criticized Roosevelt and called for the nationalization of banks and utilities. Francis E. Townsend, a retired California physician, gained a large following with his plan for every person over sixty to receive a federal pension of two hundred dollars a month. Finally, Huey P. Long, a Democratic senator from Louisiana, gained national attention with his "Share

Our Wealth" program of taxing all large incomes and giving every citizen five thousand dollars; he was viewed as a serious political rival to Roosevelt before he was assassinated in 1935.

Partly in response to the pressures created by the popularity of these three figures, in 1935 the Roosevelt initiative proposed and endorsed several important new initiatives. The National Labor Relations Act restored to workers the right of collective bargaining (this had been lost when NIRA was overturned by the Supreme Court). The Works Progress Administration was among several new relief programs that created hundreds of thousands of government jobs. Other measures raised taxes on the wealthy and increased the federal government's power to regulate banking and utilities. Perhaps the most important achievement of 1935 was the Social Security Act, which for the first time utilized the federal government to establish a system of old-age pensions, unemployment insurance, and welfare benefits.

The third phase of Roosevelt's New Deal took place after Roosevelt's landslide reelection victory in 1936—an event that inspired predictions of more great achievements by his supporters and fears of dictatorship by his opponents. Neither happened, as Roosevelt stumbled politically with his proposal to increase the size of the Supreme Court (a proposal opponents derided as a power grab). In addition, the economy stumbled with a recession in late 1937—a development that revealed to the American public that the nation still had not solved its chronic unemployment problem. Although several laws were passed in 1937 and 1938, including the Fair Labor Standards Act, which established a national minimum wage, subsequent legislative initiatives ceased as both the president and the country gave more of their attention to foreign affairs, including a war threatening in Europe.

Just as important as his proposals and programs was Roosevelt's personality. In stark contrast to his often grim-faced predecessor, Franklin D. Roosevelt conveyed an ebullient sense of optimism and hope that he was able to communicate through radio "fireside chats" as well as speeches to Congress and the public. He was the dominant political figure of his time, a fact reflected in his frequent portrayal in the political cartoons of the era. This chapter provides a small sampling of the cartoons inspired by Roosevelt and the New Deal.

Examining Cartoon 1:
"Vote for Roosevelt"

About the Cartoon

For decades after African Americans were granted suffrage follow-ing the Civil War, they had traditionally voted Republican. In the 1932 presidential election, however, some African American news-papers urged their readers to break with tradition and vote for De-mocratic presidential candidate Franklin D. Roosevelt and his running mate John Garner. This cartoon by Ollie Harrington, published in October 1932 in the black newspaper *New York State Contender*, depicts an army of black Americans leaving the "Republican wreckage" caused by the Great Depression and Republican policies to support the ticket of Roosevelt and Garner. (The sign "Light Wines and Beer" is a passing reference to another political issue of the time—the Constitution's prohibition of alcohol). Harrington's depiction was actually premature; many black Americans did switch their political support to Roosevelt, but not until 1936.

About the Cartoonist

Ollie Harrington was one of America's pioneering black cartoonists. He worked for several major African American newspapers, including the *Pittsburgh Courier* and the *Chicago Defender*. His cartoon series Dark Laughter was the first black comic strip to receive national recognition.

Examining Cartoon 2:
"Spirit of the New Deal"

About the Cartoon

One of the first and largest New Deal government agencies was the
National Recovery Adminstration (NRA). It was established to help
implement the National Industrial Recovery Act (NIRA), passed in
1933. Under NIRA, businesses were to get together and draft codes
of "fair competition" and set uniform standards for production,
prices, and wages. Businesses that agreed to abide by these codes

could display the NRA's symbol, a blue eagle, and consumers were encouraged to patronize businesses that subscribed to an NRA code. This cartoon, with its depiction of Uncle Sam and two figures representing labor and business proudly wearing the NRA symbol, is a positive depiction of the spirit of patriotic cooperation between workers and employers that the NRA was supposed to inspire.

The cartoon was drawn in July 1933, shortly after the NRA was established. Over the next several years, however, the NRA lost much of its initial popularity. Small businesses complained that the codes were biased in favor of large corporations, while businesses in general complained about government paperwork and regulation required by the law. In May 1935 the Supreme Court killed the NRA, ruling that it improperly delegated legislative powers to the executive branch of government and that it was an unconstitutional regulation of intrastate commerce.

About the Cartoonist

Clifford K. Berryman was a prolific cartoonist for the *Washington Evening Star* from 1907 until 1949, and won a Pulitzer Prize in 1944.

Examining Cartoon 3:

"I've Got the Engine Started, but . . ."

"I'VE GOT THE ENGINE STARTED, BUT . . ."

About the Cartoon

Many political arguments in the 1930s dwelt on the proper level of federal government spending and taxation. This cartoon by Herbert Johnson is a visualization of the assertion, made by many conservative opponents of President Franklin D. Roosevelt's New Deal policies, that federal taxes were too high. An embattled little "Taxpayer" (a recurring character in Johnson's work) is trying to get the boat of "Business" moving, but the fat "Tax Burden" it is carrying is making its engine useless.

About the Cartoonist

Herbert Johnson was a cartoonist for the *Saturday Evening Post*. A collection of his cartoons, many of them critical of the administration of President Franklin D. Roosevelt and the New Deal, was published in 1935.

Examining Cartoon 4:
"Boo-hoo"

About the Cartoon

By 1935 the U.S. Chamber of Commerce had come out against the New Deal as being antibusiness. Other conservative business leaders formed the American Liberty League, which was founded to oppose Roosevelt's programs as too socialistic. This 1936 cartoon juxtaposes a montage of positive newspaper articles with a picture of two stereotyped "fat cats" bemoaning the state of the country under Roosevelt's New Deal. The positive headlines and the unflattering way the two complainers are drawn suggests that the cartoonist, contrary to the president's critics, believes that the president has the country on track.

About the Cartoonist

Tom Talburt was the editorial cartoonist for the *New York Daily News*.

Examining Cartoon 5:
"The Campaign"

About the Cartoon

This cartoon was published shortly before the November 1936 presidential election, in which President Franklin D. Roosevelt was challenged by Kansas governor Alfred M. Landon. The cartoon reflects the idea that Roosevelt was engaging in unseemly class warfare in the campaign by blaming the upper class for the nation's continuing economic woes. It shows the president moving to the next campaign stop carrying his "soapbox" and a handy straw person representing entrenched greed. Despite these and other cartoons attacking Roosevelt as a "rabble rouser," he won the election by more than 11 million votes.

One interesting note is that President Roosevelt is depicted as walking unasssisted—something he never did after being stricken with polio in 1921. Virtually all the editorial cartoonists of this time refrained from drawing President Roosevelt with crutches or a wheelchair, regardless of their political beliefs.

About the Cartoonist

Hugh Hutton drew political cartoons for the *Philadelphia Inquirer*.

Examining Cartoon 6:

"Oh, the Old Gray Mare, She Ain't What She Used to Be"

About the Cartoon

The 1938 Fair Labor Standards Act, which established a national minimum wage, was the last major domestic reform of President Franklin D. Roosevelt's New Deal. The following year World War II began in Europe; America entered the conflict in December 1941. As crisis and war took up the attention of both Roosevelt and the American public, several New Deal social programs, including the Works Progress Administration and the Civilian Conservation Corps, were either dissolved or severely cut back, much to the chagrin of some Roosevelt administration officials. These leaders were further dismayed when Roosevelt in December 1943 told journalists that "Dr. New Deal" had been supplanted by "Dr. Win the War." This transition from the New Deal to World War II finds expression in this Clifford K. Berryman cartoon, first published on December 26, 1943. It shows three liberal New Deal figures—presidential adviser Harry Hopkins, Vice President Henry Wallace, and Secretary of the Interior Harold Ickes—riding an old and worn horse labeled "New Deal" and singing the popular song "Oh, the old gray mare, she ain't what she used to be." President Roosevelt argues that they need to "turn her out to pasture" and join him in his automobile labeled "Win the War."

About the Cartoonist

Clifford K. Berryman is perhaps most famous for his 1902 cartoon creating the Teddy Bear as a symbolic figure for President Theodore H. Roosevelt. He was the political cartoonist for the *Washington Post* from 1896 to 1907 and the *Washington Evening Star* from 1907 until his death in 1949. He won a Pulitzer Prize in 1944.

Chronology

November 6, 1928
Herbert Hoover is elected president.

October 24, 1929
On "Black Thursday," stock prices fall sharply as 13 million shares of stock change hands at the New York Stock Exchange.

October 29, 1929
On "Black Tuesday," Wall Street suffers the worst day in its history as investors lose $16 billion.

November 19–27, 1929
President Hoover convenes several conferences with the leaders of industry, finance, agriculture, utilities, and the Federal Reserve System, asking them to pledge to maintain employment, wages, and prices. Hoover recommends increased federal spending for public works such as dams and highways.

June 1930
Congress passes the Smoot-Hawley Tariff, sharply raising duties for numerous agricultural and industrial goods.

October 1930
Hoover forms the President's Emergency Committee for Employment. At a speech before the American Bankers Association he denounces "economic fatalists" and predicts that the "genius of American business" will restore prosperity.

December 1930
Thirteen hundred banks have failed over the course of 1930.

February 1931

"Food riots" break out in parts of the United States, including Minneapolis, where several hundred men and women loot a grocery store.

March 1931

Police and Ford company guards fire on unemployed workers marching on the Ford Motor Company's plant in River Rouge, Michigan; four workers are killed.

September 1931

Farmers in Iowa and Minnesota take matters into their own hands by forcibly blocking farm foreclosures.

December 1931

The once-powerful Bank of the United States fails, wiping out $200 million in deposits. An estimated 4.5 million Americans are unemployed.

1932–1936

A four-year drought creates the dust bowl in Texas and neighboring states, creating more hardships for farmers and farmworkers.

January 1932

President Hoover signs into law the creation of the Reconstruction Finance Corporation, allowing the expenditure of $1.5 billion to aid businesses and banks. Congressman Fiorello La Guardia denounces that legislation as a "millionaires' dole."

July 1932

The Bonus Army, a group of World War I veterans demanding early payment of cash bonuses promised for military service, is driven out of its makeshift encampment just outside of Washington, D.C., by General Douglas MacArthur on the orders of President Hoover.

November 8, 1932

Roosevelt crushes Hoover in the general presidential election.

December 1932

Unemployment in the United States reaches nearly 13 billion.

March 4, 1933

Roosevelt is inaugurated as president; his inaugural address includes the assertion "the only thing we have to fear is fear itself."

March 5, 1933

President Roosevelt declares a national bank holiday effective the following day to prevent further bank runs and closures.

March 9–June 16, 1933

The first hundred days of the New Deal. A special session of Congress called by Roosevelt results in the creation of the Federal Deposit Insurance Corporation, the National Recovery Administration, the Federal Emergency Relief Administration, the Tennessee Valley Authority, and other programs.

April 19, 1933

The United States abandons the gold standard.

Spring 1934

More than 1.5 million workers nationwide go on strike, including West Coast longshoremen, who bring docks in San Francisco and other cities to a standstill.

April 1935

Congress passes the Wealth Tax Act, providing for higher taxes on richer Americans.

May 1935

The Supreme Court declares the National Industrial Recovery Act unconstitutional, arguing that Congress has no control over intrastate commerce.

May 6, 1935

President Roosevelt issues an executive order creating the Works Progress Administration.

May 27, 1935

The Supreme Court strikes down several New Deal programs, including the National Recovery Administration, as unconstitutional.

July 5, 1935

Roosevelt signs the National Labor Relations Act into law.

August 14, 1935
The Social Security Act is signed by Roosevelt.

September 8, 1935
Louisiana's governor Huey Long, who had gained nationwide recognition for "Share the Wealth," his proposed wealth redistribution program, is assassinated.

November 9, 1935
Disaffected by the policies of the American Federation of Labor, labor leaders, including John L. Lewis of the United Mine Workers, form the Congress of Industrial Organizations.

February 1936
The Supreme Court declares the Agricultural Adjustment Act unconstitutional.

March 1936
Photographs of harvest workers by Dorothea Lange are published in the *San Francisco News*.

November 3, 1936
Roosevelt wins reelection, defeating Kansas governor Alf Landon by an electoral college margin of 523 to 8.

December 1936
The United Automobile Workers begins a sit-down strike against General Motors in Detroit.

February 5, 1937
President Roosevelt submits a proposal to expand the size of the Supreme Court; it is rejected by Congress in July.

April 1937
The American economy reaches the level of output it had reached in 1929 prior to the Great Depression.

April 12, 1937
The Supreme Court upholds the constitutionality of the National Labor Relations Act.

August 1937
America's economic recovery suffers a setback as the nation experiences a severe recession.

June 1938
Congress authorizes billions of dollars for public works projects and passes the Fair Labor Standards Act, providing for a minimum wage of forty cents an hour and a forty-hour workweek.

February 27, 1939
The Supreme Court outlaws sit-down strikes.

November 5, 1940
President Roosevelt wins a third term of office.

1941–1945
The United States fights in World War II against Germany, Japan, and Italy; the massive mobilization of labor and spending for war production helps pull the nation out of the Great Depression.

April 12, 1945
President Roosevelt dies.

For Further Research

Books

Anthony J. Badger, *The New Deal: The Depression Years, 1933–1940*. New York: Noonday, 1989.

Irving Bernstein, *The Turbulent Years*. Boston: Houghton Mifflin, 1970.

Alan Brinkley, *Voices of Protest: Huey Long, Father Coughlin, and the Great Depression*. New York: Random House, 1983.

Jay N. Darling, *As Ding Saw Herbert Hoover*. Ames: Iowa State University Press, 1996.

Kenneth Davis, *FDR: The New Deal Years, 1933–1937*. New York: Random House, 1986.

Roy Douglas, *Between the Wars, 1919–1939: The Cartoonists' Vision*. New York: Routledge, 1992.

Robert J. Hastings, *A Nickel's Worth of Skim Milk: A Boy's View of the Great Depression*. Carbondale: Southern Illinois University Press, 1972.

Stephen Hess and Milton Kaplan, *The Ungentlemanly Art: A History of American Political Cartoons*. New York: Macmillan, 1968.

Joan Hoff-Wilson, *Herbert Hoover, Forgotten Progressive*. Boston: Little, Brown, 1975.

Jan N. Jones, Jan Waskowitz, and Robert J. Norell, *We Want Jobs: A Story of the Great Depression*. New York: Raintree/Steck-Vaughn, 1992.

David M. Kennedy, *Freedom from Fear: American People in Depression and War, 1929–1945*. New York: Oxford University Press, 1999.

William E. Leuchtenburg, ed., *The New Deal: A Documentary History*. New York: Harper and Row, 1968.

Louis W. Liebovich, *Bylines in Despair: Herbert Hoover, the Great Depression, and the U.S. News Media*. Westport, CT: Praeger, 1994.

Louis Lozowick, *William Gropper*. New York: Cornwall Books, 1983.

Robert S. McElvaine, *The Great Depression: America, 1929–1941*. New York: Random House, 1985.

Robert S. McElvaine, ed., *Down and Out in the Great Depression: Letters from the "Forgotten Man."* Chapel Hill: University of North Carolina Press, 1983.

Milton Meltzer, *Brother, Can You Spare a Dime? The Great Depression, 1929–1933*. New York: New American Library, 1977.

Juliet Haines Mofford, *Talkin' Union: The American Labor Movement*. Carlisle, MA: Discovery Enterprises, 1997.

Richard H. Pells, *Radical Visions and American Dreams: Culture and Social Thought During the Depression Years*. Chicago: University of Illinois Press, 1998.

Elliot A. Rosen, *Hoover, Roosevelt, and the Brains Trust: From Depression to New Deal*. New York: Columbia University Press, 1977.

Anne E. Schraff, *The Great Depression and the New Deal: America's Economic Collapse and Recovery*. New York: Franklin Watts, 1990.

Jordan A. Schwarz, *The Interregnum of Despair: Hoover, Congress, and the Great Depression*. Urbana: University of Illinois Press, 1970.

Gilbert Seldes, *The Years of the Locust: America, 1929–1932*. Boston: Little, Brown, 1933.

Harvard Sitkoff, *A New Deal for Blacks*. New York: Oxford University Press, 1978.

Gene Smith, *The Shattered Dream; Herbert Hoover and the Great Depression*. New York: Morrow, 1970.

Harvey Swados, ed., *The American Writer and the Great Depression*. Indianapolis: Bobbs-Merrill, 1966.

Studs Terkel, *Hard Times: An Oral History of the Great Depression*. New York: Random House, 1970.

Errol Lincoln Uys, *Riding the Rails: Teenagers on the Move During the Great Depression*. New York: Penguin, 1993.

Timothy Walch and Dwight M. Miller, *Herbert Hoover and Franklin D. Roosevelt: A Documentary History*. Westport, CT: Greenwood, 1998.

Geoffrey C. Ward, *A First-Class Temperament: The Emergence of Franklin Roosevelt*. New York: Harper and Row, 1989.

T.H. Watkins, *The Great Depression: America in the 1930s*. Boston: Little, Brown, 1993.

———, *The Hungry Years: A Narrative History of the Great Depression in America*. New York: Henry Holt, 1999.

Betty Houchin Winfield, *FDR and the News Media*. New York: Columbia University Press, 1994.

George Wolfskill, *Revolt of the Conservatives: A History of the American Liberty League, 1934–1940*. Boston: Houghton Mifflin, 1962.

George Wolfskill and John A. Hudson, *All but the People: Franklin D. Roosevelt and His Critics*. New York: Macmillan, 1969.

Richard Wormser, *Growing Up in the Great Depression*. New York: Atheneum, 1995.

Websites

FDR Cartoon Archive, www.nisk.k12.ny.us/fdr. The website features an extensive collection of political cartoons on President Franklin Delano Roosevelt that have been digitized.

Hoover Online! Digital Archives, www.ecommcode.com/hoover/hooveronline/index.html. Part of the Hoover Presidential Library, this website serves as an electronic research room that can furnish students with direct access to materials held at the library, including political cartoons.

New Deal Network, http://newdeal.feri.org/. The website is an educational guide to the Great Depression that is sponsored by the Franklin and Eleanor Roosevelt Institute and the Institute for Learning Technologies at Teachers College/Columbia University. It includes photographs, primary source documents, and lesson plans covering various aspects of the Great Depression.

Index

African Americans
  support for Roosevelt among, 54–55
  unemployment among, 10, 23
Agricultural Adjustment Administration (AAA), 16, 17, 51–52
American Liberty League, 52, 61

bank failures, 22, 31, 34
bank holiday, 51
Banking Act (1935), 17
Berryman, Clifford K., 57, 65
Billington, Ray Allen, 11
Brinkley, Alan, 18, 51
business investment, fall in, 10, 33

Carver, Thomas N., 9
Chase, Stuart, 14
Civilian Conservation Corps (CCC), 16, 65
Civil Works Administration (CWA), 16
consumer spending, fall in, 33
Coolidge, Calvin, 8, 33
Coughlin, Charles, 52

Darling, Jay Norwood ("Ding"), 40
dockworkers strike, 49
Duffy, Edmund, 27, 36
dust bowl, 23

election of 1932, 14, 15, 51
Emergency Banking Act (1933), 51

Fair Labor Standards Act (1938), 53, 65
farmers, 35–36
  effects of depression on, 23
  1920s economy and, 12
Federal Deposit Insurance Corporation (FDIC), 16
Federal Emergency Relief Administration (FERA), 16
Federal Home Loan Banks, 40
Federal Reserve Board, 17
fireside chats, 17
Fitzpatrick, Daniel, 29
Flynn, John T., 17
Ford, Henry, 47

Garner, John, 55
Girdler, Tom, 47

Great Depression
  rural effects of, 23
  social effects of, 19
Gropper, William, 47
gross national product (GNP),
  in 1920s, 8

Harding, Warren G., 8, 33
Harrington, Ollie, 55
Home Owners Loan Corpora-
  tion (HOLC), 16
Hoover, Herbert, 9, 10
  declares moratorium on
    payment of foreign debt
    to U.S., 36
  optimistic predictions of,
    37–38
  on public relief, 12–13
  response of, to economic
    downturn, 11–13, 26–27,
    33–34
Hoovervilles, 13, 34
Hopkins, Harry, 65
Hudson, John A., 19
Hutton, Hugh, 63

Ickes, Harold, 65

Johnson, Herbert, 58, 59

Kirby, Rollin, 38

labor unions, 42
  growth of, 43, 47
Landon, Alfred M., 63
Leuchtenburg, William, 9
Lewis, Ross A., 49
Liebovich, Louis W., 11
Long, Huey P., 52–53

McCutcheon, John T., 24, 25,
  31
minimum wage, establishment
  of, 53
Morison, Samuel Elliot, 18

National Industrial Recovery
  Act (1933), 52, 56
  Supreme Court strikes down,
    42
National Labor Relations Act
  (1935), 42, 53
National Labor Relations
  Board (NLRB), 42–43
National Recovery Administration (NRA), 16, 17,
  56–57
New Deal
  achievements of, 17–19
  opposition to, 61
  phases of, 51–53
  programs of, 16–17
  transition to World War II
    from, 65
New Masses (journal), 13
1920s
  antiunion efforts in, 42
  economy of, 8–9
  poverty in, 12
Norris–La Guardia Anti-
  Injunction Act (1932), 42

Pease, Lute, 45
Pells, Richard H., 14, 34
Perkins, Frances, 14
poverty, in 1920s, 12

Reconstruction Finance
  Corporation (RFC), 34, 40

Roosevelt, Franklin D., 10
    depiction of, 63
    fireside chats of, 17
    first inaugural address of,
        15–16
    New Deal and, 16–17
    1932 elections and, 14
    support for, among African
        Americans, 54–55

Securities and Exchange
    Commission (SEC), 17
Sinclair, Upton, 13
sit-down strikes, 43
socialism, as alternative to
    capitalism, 13–14
Social Security Act (1935), 17,
    53
stock market
    1920s boom in, 8
    1929 crash of, 9–10, 27
        effects on consumers, 22–23

effects on U.S. banks, 22
    Hoover's response to, 11–12
strikes, labor, 42, 43, 49
suicides, 11
Supreme Court
    Roosevelt's attempt to
        enlarge, 53
    strikes down New Deal
        programs, 42, 52, 57

Talburt, Tom, 61
Townsend, Francis E., 52

unemployment
    New Deal and changes in, 18
    rise in, 10, 23, 33

Wallace, Henry, 65
Wilson, Edmund, 13
Wolfskill, George, 19
Works Progress Administration
    (WPA), 16, 65